International Food Library

FOOD IN
INDIA

International Food Library

FOOD IN
INDIA

Sharon Kaur

Rourke Publications, Inc.
Vero Beach, Florida 32964

Library of Congress Cataloging-in-Publication Data

Kaur, Sharon, 1948-
   Food in India/by Sharon Kaur.
     p. cm. - (International food)
   Includes index.
   Summary: Surveys food products, customs, and preparation in India, describing regional dishes, cooking techniques, and recipes for a variety of meals.
   ISBN 0-86625-339-4
   1. Cookery, India - Juvenile literature. 2. Food habits - India - Juvenile literature. [1. Cookery, India. 2. Food habits - India. 3. India - Social life and customs.] I. Title. II. Series.
TX724.5.I4K315   1989
394. 1'0954-dc19   88-31294
                CIP
                AC

CONTENTS

AN INTRODUCTION TO INDIA

India's triangular land mass is divided into three main geographic areas. The high mountains of the Himalayas in the far north fall abruptly to the plains, where the great River Ganges and its tributaries flow steadily eastward. To the south, the uplands of the Deccan plateau push out into the Indian Ocean.

The Indian Republic is a union of 25 states and 7 centrally administered union territories including the Andaman and Nicobar Islands. This land of 1¼ million square miles is a country of contrast. India's terrain varies from lush rain forest in the southwest to fertile alluvial plains along the rivers, to barren desert on the northwest border with Pakistan.

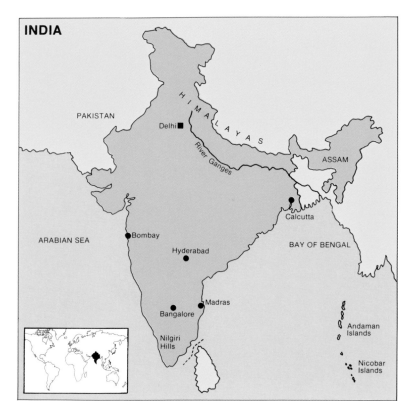

India is a country of great contrast; this peaceful scene is typical of many parts of southern India.

India has a population of nearly 800 million, which is growing at the incredible rate of one million per month. One-third of India's people live in the densely populated capital city, Delhi, and the Ganges Valley states of Uttar Pradesh, Bihar, and West Bengal. Other major cities include Hyderabad, Bangalore, and the great ports of Bombay, Calcutta, and Madras.

India's history can be traced back to around 2,500 B.C., when northwest and west India was settled by people of the Harappa culture. Their towns were well laid out, with good streets, public baths, large houses for the rich, and smaller dwellings for their servants. The Harappa people cultivated rice, wheat, and cotton, as well as peas and sesame.

India's agriculture developed steadily over the years. The introduction of iron tools around 1,000 B.C. helped the people clear the forests and cultivate more land. By about 700 A.D. farming had spread to the drier areas, where a good supply of water was needed. Over the next centuries, an impressive irrigation system was built, using water wheels and tanks or reservoirs; many of the tanks are still used today.

AGRICULTURE IN INDIA

By the end of this century, India's population will have grown to nearly one billion. Until now, the country has almost always been able to grow enough rice and wheat to feed its population without having to import food. India places great importance on keeping rice and wheat production high enough to maintain this self-sufficiency through the turn of the century. It also hopes to become self-sufficient in such pulses (seeds of certain plants) as mung beans and such oilseeds as groundnut, and to be able to export more fish, fruit, vegetables, and spices.

Farmers in India face some unique problems. Because India's population is rising, the area of land under cultivation is being sharply reduced as the demand for new housing, roads, and industry is met. The land itself, though fertile in many parts, is often dry with thin topsoil. Drought, floods, fire, and earthquakes are common in India and can ruin crops without warning. Additionally, in this huge country with over two hundred languages, communication can be difficult.

Fishing provides food for many people who live along India's long coastline. These fishermen are hauling in their day's catch.

Much agricultural work is done by hand. This woman is reaping corn in the foothills of the Himalayas.

The Indian government has a series of programs aimed at modernizing the country's agriculture. The use of fertilizers and pesticides is actively encouraged, and they are offered at affordable prices. Irrigation is being improved and extended into new areas. Good quality seeds are vital. Some kinds are specially developed for certain climatic and soil conditions, and distributed to farmers throughout India.

The government offers advice and training for growing new crops. In the 1970s, satellite data was used to study growing conditions and crop disease. A United Nations program helped broadcast agricultural information to every village throughout India in many different languages.

FOOD IN INDIA

The staple foods in India are rice and wheat. These are supplemented by many kinds of lentils, vegetables, meat, and fish, most of which are farmed locally. Milk products like yogurt, curd, and clarified butter, called *ghee*, are often used in traditional Indian cooking.

Indians make several kinds of breads with whole wheat or corn flour. These breads, eaten hot, are popular with almost any meal. They are prepared in a variety of ways — baked in an oven, cooked on a griddle, or fried. Most Indian breads are unleavened, and are flat and round like thick pancakes. One kind, called a *chapati*, is a favorite accompaniment to Indian curries.

Indian curries are always spicy, but they are not always the hot, fiery dishes that some people expect. Many curries contain neither chilies nor hot peppery ingredients. A combination of traditionally used herbs, spices, and seasonings will produce an interesting and tasty meal that can be readily identified as Indian.

Over one hundred different spices are used in Indian cooking, and only a few of them are hot. The most commonly used spice is a dark yellow powder called turmeric, which gives curries a yellowish color and a light, fragrant taste. Commercial curry powder bought in supermarkets should never be used in true Indian

Fresh vegetables are abundant in most parts of India.

10

An Indian woman displays a tray of beautifully made breads and cookies.

cooking. Different spices in varying quantities are needed for each dish; commercial curry powder makes everything taste the same.

A typical Indian family meal consists of a fish or meat curry, two or three vegetable dishes, rice or lentils, Indian bread, and a choice of chutneys or pickles. These savory dishes are followed by a dessert and possibly some fresh fruit.

11

BEANS, PEAS, AND LENTILS

India is the world's leading producer of pulses, which are the seeds of certain plants. Around sixty different types are cultivated, including mung beans, soy beans, green and yellow lentils, chick peas, and black-eyed peas. Pulses are one of India's principal crops, accounting for one-fifth of its crop production. But to keep up with the increasing population, this production must increase by over one-third by the end of the century.

Quick-growing mung beans are grown throughout India. In several states farmers have been encouraged to cultivate extra mung beans in the summer months, in between their other crops. The summer mung is sown immediately after the spring harvest of potatoes, wheat, and sugar cane. It is harvested before the farmers need to plant the following year's crops.

This street vendor in Bombay is selling beans and lentils.

Baisen flour is used to make many different kinds of Indian breads.

This extra cultivation has more than doubled India's production of mung beans over the last few years. It also has another advantage. Mung beans are leguminous plants that are rich in nitrates, chemicals that plants draw from the soil to help them grow. The mung bean crop puts nitrates back into the soil, and they feed the next crop.

Pulses are an excellent source of vegetable protein, and are very important in the Indian diet. They are eaten in many different ways. The beans and lentils can be boiled in the same way as rice, perhaps with vegetables and meat, or they can be roasted or fried in spices to make delicious, crunchy snacks. Split black chick peas are ground into baisen flour and used to make breads and batters. Newly sprouting mung beans are popular as a salad vegetable.

13

TEA

India's tea industry was first developed in the mid-nineteenth century, when the British began to plant tea bushes smuggled out of China. By the early 1900s India's tea plantations were firmly established, and the country is now the largest tea producer in the world. Indian tea is exported to Europe, North America, and the U.S.S.R.

The main tea-growing areas are the states of Assam and West Bengal in northeast India. These two states produce more than three-quarters of India's tea. There are also important tea plantations in the Nilgiri Hills in the south Indian state of Tamil Nadu and in neighboring Kerala.

These girls are tea pickers in the northern Indian state of Assam.

A tea plantation from above.

Tea bushes grow best in fairly warm, humid climates that are free from frost. In an Indian plantation, the bushes are normally grown from seed in sheltered nurseries. Six months later, when the plants are about six or eight inches tall, they are planted out in neat rows in the fields. The bushes are left to grow for two years, when they are pruned from their height of five or six feet down to just one foot. The trees reach maturity at the end of the third year, and their bright green shoots are ready for picking.

Tea leaves can be processed in three different ways to produce green, black or oolong teas. India produces mostly black tea. After picking, the tea leaves are dried in the sun for one day before they are rolled to release all their juices. The leaves are then put into baskets, covered with damp cloths, and left for a couple of hours to ferment. After the final drying stage, the leaves are ready for packing.

REGIONAL COOKING

As one would expect in so large a country, India has a great variety of regional foods and cooking methods. Ingredients do not only differ according to availability, though. In India, religion and caste are leading influences on people's diets.

Long ago, Indian society was organized into four castes, or classes — *Brahmins* (priests and teachers), *Kshatriyas* (warriors and chiefs), *Vaishyas* (traders and farmers) and *Shudras* (unskilled workers). The top two castes, the *Brahmins* and *Kshatriyas*, were usually vegetarians, while the lower castes ate meat. While the caste structure is less rigid today, it still plays a leading role in Indian society and culture. Indian eating habits are further divided by religion. The Muslim community does not eat pork, which it considers unclean. Hindus do not eat beef, since cows are sacred to their religion.

Because of these religious differences, lamb and chicken are the most popular meats in Indian cooking. In certain areas, of course, pork and beef are also eaten. Pork vindaloo, a hot and vinegary dish, and pork-based sausages are specialties of the west coast state of Goa.

Far in the north of India, this man is making yogurt. Yogurt is an important ingredient in north Indian cooking.

Holy men of the Brahmin class do not eat meat.

In general, the foods of south India are hotter and spicier than those of the north. Local produce such as coconuts, cashew nuts, and an herb called curry leaf are commonly used, and all meals are served with rice.

Northern recipes are sweeter and milder. They call for a liberal use of cream, curd, and almonds, introduced into the region's cuisine by the great Moghul emperors of the sixteenth and seventeenth centuries. Meats cooked in a clay oven, in a style called *tandoori*, originated in the north, but are found throughout India today.

17

INDIAN FESTIVALS

Each year over fifty major festivals are celebrated throughout India. Other regional festivities add to that number, and hardly a day goes by without a celebration somewhere in the country!

Most of the festivals have religious origins. Some are Hindu, while others are Buddhist, Muslim, or Christian. Certain celebrations, like Independence Day and Republic Day, commemorate the union of the Indian states into one independent nation. Some festivals celebrate the changing seasons, harvests, local deities, and marriages. Whatever the occasion, you may be sure to find brightly colored costumes, markets, flowers, fruit, magicians, elephants, music, dancing, singing, and a good deal of fun.

This beautiful picture made of flowers shows the Hindu god Sri Ayapa who is popular in southern India.

Women at the religious festival of Ramoripuna in Bombay.

Hindu religious festivals are the most colorful and are fascinating to watch. Some, like *Navratri*, last for several days. Images of Hindu gods and goddesses are worshiped in every home, while for nine successive nights *Ramalila* is acted out through music and dance. *Ramilila* is a traditional story that tells of the Hindu god-king Rama's battle against evil. The bad king Ravana represents the evil spirits. On the tenth night, Rama's victory over the evil spirits is celebrated with firecrackers and burning likenesses of Ravana, to keep away evil for the coming year.

Islamic festivals are generally more serious, centering around prayers and worship at the mosques. For one month each year, during a special time called *Ramadan*, Muslims are not allowed to eat during daylight hours. At the end of *Ramadan* new clothes are bought, and after prayers at the mosques families and friends gather together for great celebration dinners.

19

A BANQUET MENU FOR A FESTIVE OCCASION

Chicken Tikka
Shrimp With Mint
Mushroom Curry
Spicy Chick Peas
Cucumber Chutney
Boiled Rice
Selection Of Fresh Fruit

At an Indian banquet, all the savory dishes are normally served at the same time. Begin with the Chicken Tikka, continuing with the other recipes while that is marinating for 4 hours. Serve a selection of fresh fruit for dessert. The recipes are designed to serve six people. Use 2 cups of uncooked rice for the boiled rice.

Chicken Tikka

  1 lb. boned chicken, cut into 1 inch cubes
  2 onions, cut into quarters
  1 tablespoon minced ginger root
  1 teaspoon minced garlic
  2 tablespoons finely chopped coriander leaves
  ½ teaspoon turmeric powder
  ½ teaspoon salt
    juice of 2 lemons
  1 tablespoon oil or ghee
  ½ cup plain unsweetened yogurt
  6 skewers

1. Marinate the chicken in the lemon juice for 15 minutes.
2. Mix together the ginger, garlic, coriander leaves, turmeric, salt, oil or ghee, and yogurt. Add to the chicken and lemon juice. Cover and marinate for 4 hours.
3. Thread alternate pieces of onion and chicken onto the skewers. These are called kebabs.
4. Grill the chicken and onion kebabs on an outdoor barbecue grill over very hot coals, or place in an oven under the broiler. Using a hot

Chicken Tikka.

pad, turn the kebabs every few mintues, until brown and thoroughly cooked. Serve hot.

Shrimp With Mint

l lb. large shrimp, shelled
1 onion, chopped
3 tomatoes, chopped
¼ cup oil or ghee
½ cup fresh mint, chopped
½ teaspoon turmeric
½ teaspoon chili powder
1 teaspoon salt

1. Heat half the oil in a large pan and fry the shrimp over a fairly high heat for 2 minutes. Remove from the pan and set to one side.
2. Heat the remaining oil and fry the onion until golden brown. Add the tomatoes, turmeric, chili powder, and salt and cook gently for 2 minutes.
3. Return the shrimp to the pan and stir in the mint. Cook gently for 8 minutes and serve hot.

Mushroom Curry

½ lb. whole button mushrooms
1 onion, chopped
1 tomato, chopped
1 tablespoon oil or ghee
1 teaspoon salt
1 teaspoon minced root ginger
½ teaspoon chili powder
¼ teaspoon turmeric
⅓ cup water
2 tablespoons chopped coriander leaves

1. Heat the oil or ghee in a pan and fry the onion and ginger until soft.
2. Add the mushrooms, tomato, water, salt, and spices. Cover and cook gently for 5 minutes.
3. Sprinkle with coriander before serving.

Spicy Chick Peas

2 cups canned chick peas
2 tablespoons oil or ghee
1 onion, finely chopped
1 small green chili, finely chopped
1 teaspoon minced garlic
1 teaspoon minced root ginger
1 teaspoon cinnamon powder
1 teaspoon cumin seeds
½ teaspoon turmeric
½ teaspoon salt
1 cardamom seed
3 cloves
1 teaspoon cornstarch
1 cup water
juice of ½ lemon
2 tablespoons fresh coriander leaves, finely chopped

Shrimp with mint.

1. Heat the oil or ghee in a pan and gently fry the onion, garlic, ginger, and chili for 3 minutes. Add the chick peas, salt, and spices and fry for 1 minute.
2. Mix the cornstarch and water and pour into the pan. Cook over a low heat for 15 minutes.
3. Stir in the lemon juice and coriander leaves just before serving.

Cucumber Chutney

   1 cucumber, finely chopped
   ¼ green chili pepper, finely chopped
   ½ teaspoon salt
   1 teaspoon chopped coriander leaves
      juice of ½ lemon

1. Mix all ingredients together in a bowl and let stand for 30 minutes. Served chilled.

A SOUTH INDIAN MEAL

Southern Style Fish Curry
Rice With Peas

This south Indian meal is quick and easy to prepare. Begin with the rice, and while that is cooking make the fish curry. If the rice is ready a little before the curry, keep it warm in an oven preheated to 350 degrees. Serve both dishes at the same time.

Southern Style Fish Curry

1½ lb. white fish fillets, sliced
½ cup coconut milk
½ cup water
1 large onion, chopped
3 tomatoes, chopped
2 tablespoon oil or ghee
1 red chili, seeded and finely chopped
1 green chili, seeded and finely chopped
1 tablespoon minced ginger root
2 bay leaves
   juice of 1 lemon
½ teaspoon salt
1 teaspoon fenugreek powder
1 teaspoon coriander powder
1 teaspoon cumin seeds

1. Heat the oil or ghee in a large pan and fry the onion, bay leaves, red and green chilies, and ginger for 2 minutes. Add the tomatoes, salt, and spices and fry gently for 1 minute.
2. Stir in the fish pieces, coconut milk, and water. Cover and cook for 15 minutes.
3. Add the lemon juice just before serving.

Southern style fish curry.

Rice With Peas

1½ cups long-grain rice
¾ cup green peas (fresh or frozen)
2 tablespoons oil or ghee
½ onion, finely chopped
1 teaspoon cumin seeds
3 cups hot water
1 teaspoon salt

1. Soak the rice in 6 cups of water for 30 minutes. Drain.
2. Heat the oil or ghee in a pan and fry the cumin seeds and chopped onion. Add the rice and peas and stir for 2 minutes.
3. Pour in the 3 cups of hot water and add the salt. Cover and cook for 20 minutes. Drain.

A NORTH INDIAN MEAL

Lamb Curry With Almonds
Chapatis

This traditional curry has a mild flavor, sweetened by honey and delicate spices. Make the *chapatis* while the curry is slowly cooking for one hour, and serve both dishes at the same time.

Lamb Curry With Almonds

  1 lb. lamb, cut into 1 inch cubes
  3 tablespoons oil or ghee
  1 cup plain unsweetened yogurt
  ¼ cup meat stock
  1 onion, chopped
  1 tablespoon honey
  1 cup toasted almond flakes
  1 tablespoon coconut flakes
  2 teaspoons minced garlic
  1 teaspoon minced ginger root
  1 teaspoon salt
  ¼ teaspoon turmeric
  ¼ teaspoon cinnamon
  ¼ teaspoon coriander powder
  ¼ teaspoon chili powder
  4 cloves
  2 cardamoms

1. Mix the cubed lamb with 1 teaspoon minced garlic, turmeric, ginger, and yogurt in a bowl. Cover and let marinate, or soak, for four hours.
2. When the lamb is ready, heat the oil or ghee in a large pan and fry the second teaspoon of minced garlic, onion, salt and remaining spices for 2 minutes.
3. Add the lamb and yogurt mixture, stir in the coconut and meat stock, and cook gently for one hour.
4. Just before serving, stir in the honey. Serve sprinkled with toasted almonds.

Lamb Curry with Almonds.

Chapatis

> *3 cups whole wheat flour*
> *1 cup water*
> *1 teaspoon salt*
> *extra flour for kneading dough*

1. Sift the flour and salt together into a large bowl and make a well in the center.
2. Pour the water a little at a time into the well and, using a wooden spoon, work into the flour to make a soft dough. Knead the dough, using your hands, for about 5 minutes, until no longer sticky. Cover with a damp cloth and leave for 30 minutes.
3. Shape the dough into 12 balls and roll each one in a little flour until flat and about 6 inches in diameter.
4. Heat a frying pan (a cast-iron skillet works well) and put in a piece of dough. Turn the *chapati* over when the underside is slightly browned. Using a clean cloth, press the dough down firmly into the pan, and it will puff up a little. Cook until golden brown, then turn the chapati over again and brown the other side.
5. Cook the *chapatis* one by one, as above, stacking them in an oven preheated to 250 degrees as they are done. Serve hot, as soon as possible.

AN EVERYDAY MEAL

Curry and rice is a popular Indian meal. This simple chicken curry serves four people.

Chicken Curry And Rice

4 chicken legs or breasts
1 medium onion, peeled and chopped
1 tablespoon oil or ghee
1 teaspoon minced garlic
l teaspoon minced ginger root
2 green cardamom seeds
½ teaspoon turmeric
1 teaspoon paprika
¼ teaspoon chili powder
1 teaspoon salt
¾ cup water
½ cup plain unsweetened yogurt
* juice of 1 lemon*
* 2 tablespoons chopped parsley or coriander*

1. Heat the oil or ghee in a large pan and add the garlic, ginger, onion, and cardamom seeds. Fry for 2 minutes.
2. Add the chicken and fry until lightly browned.
3. Stir in the turmeric, paprika, chili powder, and salt and fry for 1 more minute. Add the water and cook gently for 30 minutes or until the chicken is cooked, stirring occasionally.
4. Just before serving, stir in the yogurt and lemon juice. Garnish with fresh parsley or coriander leaves, and serve with plain, boiled rice.

GLOSSARY OF COOKING TERMS

For those readers who are less experienced in the kitchen, the following list explains the cooking terms used in this book.

Boned	Having had the bones removed.
Chopped	Cut into small pieces measuring about ½ inch
Finely chopped	Cut into very small pieces measuring about ⅛ inch
Garnish	Decorate
Knead	To work together, using one's hands
Marinated	Covered with a mixture of juices, called a marinade, and left to soak
Minced	Chopped into tiny pieces or put through a mincer
Preheated	Already heated to the required temperature
Seeded	Having had the seeds removed
Skewers	Pointed metal or wooden sticks that hold pieces of meat or vegetables in a row
Sliced	Cut into pieces that show part of the original shape of the vegetable
Spoon measurements	Tablespoons and teaspoons should be filled only to the level of the spoons' edge, not heaped.

INDIAN COOKING

For the recipes in this book, the following items and ingredients will be necessary:

Coconut milk   Canned coconut milk can be bought at some supermarkets and specialty stores.

Ghee   Ghee, or clarified butter, is commonly used in Indian cooking. It can be made by melting 2 lbs. butter in a heavy saucepan and cooking gently for 40 minutes. The melted butter will then look clearer. While still hot, pour it through a fine cloth such as muslin into a container. Ghee will keep for about one year. Ghee, like butter, is high in cholesterol.

Ginger root   Fresh ginger can be bought in small pieces at most supermarkets.

Herbs   Bay leaves, coriander, and mint are all best if used fresh. You may be able to buy them fresh from a specialty store or farmer's market. If not, substitute dried herbs or a different fresh herb.

Oil   If you do not want to go to the trouble of making your own ghee, use olive oil or sunflower oil instead. Neither of these oils contains any cholesterol. If you are serving someone, such as a parent or a grandparent, who is on a low-cholesterol diet, be sure to use olive oil or sunflower oil instead of ghee.

Spices   Cardamom seeds, cumin seeds, cloves, and powdered spices like turmeric, paprika, chili, cinnamon, coriander, and fenugreek are available at most large supermarkets.

INDEX

We would like to thank and acknowledge the following people for the use of their photographs and transparencies:

Anthony Blake Photo Library Ltd: 24; Ardea London Ltd (J M Labat): 30; Audience Planners: Cover 10/11; Bruce Coleman Ltd (Michael Freeman): T/Page, 8; (Gerald Cubitt): 9; (David C. Houston): 12; (Jaroslav Poncar): 13; (Mark Boulton): 16; (Jonathan T Wright): 17; (Charles Henneghien): 18/19; Ebury Press: 28, 25; Lare Foods Limited: 27, 21; Octopus Book Ltd: 19; The Tea Council: Cover, 14, 15.